The Life of a
Musician

The Life of a Musician

A Musician's Perspective

LENNOX A. FERGUSON

This book is a work of non-fiction. Unless otherwise noted, the author and the publisher make no explicit guarantees as to the accuracy of the information contained in this book and in some cases, names of people and places have been altered to protect their privacy.

Archway Publishing books may be ordered through booksellers or by contacting:

Archway Publishing
1663 Liberty Drive
Bloomington, IN 47403
www.archwaypublishing.com
844-669-3957

Because of the dynamic nature of the Internet, any web addresses or links contained in this book may have changed since publication and may no longer be valid. The views expressed in this work are solely those of the author and do not necessarily reflect the views of the publisher, and the publisher hereby disclaims any responsibility for them.

Any people depicted in stock imagery provided by Getty Images are models, and such images are being used for illustrative purposes only. Certain stock imagery © Getty Images.

ISBN: 978-1-6657-1433-4 (sc)
ISBN: 978-1-6657-1431-0 (hc)
ISBN: 978-1-6657-1432-7 (e)

Library of Congress Control Number: 2021921730

Print information available on the last page.

Archway Publishing rev. date: 11/23/2021

Contents

Preface

Throughout my entire life, I have been involved in music and helping others to achieve their dreams in this field. As a result, I have gained valuable experience that has shaped and continues to shape my musical ability.

I studied percussion at the Jamaica School of Music, to which I received a full scholarship. Then I studied jazz at Nyack Christian College, where I majored in piano. I also studied at the New School for Jazz and Contemporary Arts in New York City, where I majored in jazz piano performance. I've been the music and arts director of various churches and projects, where I've managed teams of over two hundred people in my department alone, including children, teens, and adults. And I've been blessed to tour the world, playing for different artists.

Studying music has given me great insight, whether it be

through different styles of playing, playing by ear, or making tracks for studio projects. This musical experience has also allowed me to meet many people of different nationalities. Thus, I have become better able to appreciate people and their cultural expression as well as what they can bring musically to the table. As a result of these experiences, I have gained the ability to function effectively and appreciate music in all forms, styles, and genres. I can also address the concerns that keep us wondering, *Will I make it? Will I become successful?* I do believe that I speak on behalf of those who have walked this road and have survived the twists, turns, and ups and downs. I hope those of you who have had the battle marks can attest, and for those who are looking and wondering, I hope you will find what you are seeking. I am confident that my book will bring you an experience that will be a memorable one.

Chapter 1

What Is Music?

M usic is said to be an art of sound in time that expresses ideas and emotions in significant forms through the elements of rhythm, harmony, and color. But from my experience, I think that music is based on more than rhythm and harmony; the individual must make investing in him- or herself a priority in order to be fully fluent in the world of music.

According to biblical history, music has been around since before the creation of humanity. Before there was even a need for humans, music was present. Before there was a need for salvation, music was present. Before there were preachers and teachers and scholars, music was present. Before there was even a Bible or a book of law, music was present. Music is *more*. "More than what?" you may ask. Music is more than everything. I believe that music has the ability to amalgamate everything that exists within our world of life. Music is the only element on the earth that was not created on the earth. Everything that you can physically see, touch, and feel was made on this planet—the air we breathe, the trees, the water, the light, the animals, the insects, and humankind. This proves to me that music operates on a whole different scale. It is not just a tool for entertainment or to make us feel good; music is more. Music cannot be tuned out. It goes beyond the physical, the spiritual, and your soul.

If we are honest, we know songs we don't even like, and not because they were taught to us. Just by the mere fact we heard them, they got deep within us. I think it's safe to say that music is the oldest pillar of art. It existed before any history or record could be formed.

Lucifer, who was one of the archangels in heaven, is said to be the one who covered the throne. Not only did he cover the throne, but he was also placed in charge of music. In Ezekiel 28:13, you see a little bit of who Lucifer is:

> Thou had been in Eden the garden of God; every precious stone was thy covering, the stardust, topaz, and the diamond, the beryl, onyx and the jasper, the sapphire and the emerald, and the carbuncle and gold: the workmanship

of thy tabret, and of thy pipes that was created
in thee in the day that thou was created.

Biblical scholars suggest that one of the main reasons that Lucifer was created was to make music or, in other words, to usher in the presence of God. So you see, music even predates humanity. The end of the verse supports his creation; the pipes in him are for music. Music has been around longer than we can ever imagine. I also think it is safe to say that Lucifer was the first ever musician, since his role was to usher in worship and his physical makeup was created to make music.

"So what does it mean to be a musician?" you may ask. Being a musician is a lifestyle. It requires commitment to long nights of practicing the same thing over and over. It requires consistency, longevity, and learning new musical materials. Also, being a musician means making music. It's as simple as that.

The beautiful thing about music is that it is not confined to an instrument or an individual. Music is all around us. If you'll only listen, you will hear melodies around you—the wind, the birds, the wave that pulls to and fro. Music is everywhere. Music is a world all by itself. It has its own laws, structure, literature, and language. I believe that music is the most influential, liberating, and dominant force ever known to humanity. And because of this, humans have always used music to advance themselves.

One example is the way our military gives drills and

marching patterns based on songs and rhythmic patterns. When a platoon is marching, you usually hear them singing a song in a call-and-response form or a command with a rhythm to it, such as "Left, left, left, right, left." Another example of a practical use of music can be seen in the way we teach and learn—for example, our alphabet song or when we learn our timetables and our numbers. It has become a crucial tool in developing our minds to understand the fundamentals of language, science, math, arts, and history, which are essential in defining a race and its culture. Not only has it brought advancement to the human race, but it also brings health and life, both spiritually and physically.

We are in a time when music acts as a catalyst that dictates what mood to be in. Think about it: if you would like someone to get angry, you could play music that is aggressive, and if the person really listened to it, he or she could become angry. The same thing is done with happy music, sad music, and so on. If you don't believe me, go watch a movie. Pay attention to any dramatic part, and then listen to see if there is not music in the background that supports the mood or feeling that the movie wants you to experience. Or listen to any advertisement or infomercial; are there any without music to support the mood the advertiser wants the viewer to feel or experience? If you should attend a Pentecostal church, you will see that the musical makeup of the service is broken up into three segments: praise and worship, offering, and altar call. A different type of music fits each of the three segments to make them effective. And based on the choice of music, you can kind of predetermine the behavior of the people who hear it, which we will get into later on.

On another note, music therapy has grown in ways we could never have imagined. Music therapy consists of a musician using music to address issues in an individual's life and get positive results. These areas may include social, emotional, physical, aesthetic, mental, or spiritual aspects of one's life. Music therapy really stands out when it's used to help with your cognitive functions, emotional development, social skills, motor skills, and quality of life. This only proves that music and learning go hand in hand. As a matter of fact, it is essential to immerse your kids in musical activities from a young age because music supports their cognitive development. To help you to understand how big and influential music is in this area, I did a little research on cognition.

Cognition is the mental process of acquiring knowledge and understanding through thought, experience, and the senses. It encircles the course of action, such as obtaining knowledge, focusing attention, enhancing long-term and working memory, making judgments and evaluations, reasoning and computing, solving problems, making decisions, and comprehending and producing language. And music affects most, if not all, of the areas of cognition. Now, some may disagree with me and argue that it is cognition that affects music and not the other way around. But I like to think that either way, music is involved. Whether cognition affects music or music affects cognition, music still affects us. And this is my thought: Yes, I do think cognition affects the way we play music and the way we interpret music. But I also think music influences the cognitive part of the brain. Have you ever heard of a prodigy? According to dictionary.com, a prodigy is "a person, especially a child or a young person, having extraordinary talent or ability." I have seen and heard of kids showing talents and skills before they knew how to creep, walk, or talk, before they knew how to understand—all these fall under cognition. There are kids doing the unexplainable for their ages. And this does not only apply to musicians. So this is why I do believe it affects your cognition.

Music also utilizes your motor skills. The motor skills are said to be "a learned ability to cause a predetermined movement outcome with maximum certainty." The purpose of the motor skills is to optimize the ability to perform a skill successfully, with precision, and to reduce the energy consumption required for the performance.

Now, any musician's motors skills are a core part of his or her musicianship. There are three stages to motor learning: the cognitive phase, the associative phase, and the autonomous phase. The cognitive phase deals with receiving brand-new information, and the goal is to find out what needs to be done in order to execute it. So a lot of cognitive activity has to take place in order for the learner to identify the correct strategies to gain the desired goal at hand. The good strategies are saved, the bad ones are discarded, and your performance improves in a short time. So, for example, when you learn a new vocal exercise or a new scale or progression, in the cognitive phase, your mind goes through what you are expected to do. Then it goes through different strategies in order to get the best results for the warmup or for doing your scales and saves the good strategies. This is how our minds work.

The associative phase kicks in next. The associative phase happens after the learner has found the best or most effective way to execute the goal. He or she makes minor adjustments in the performance. Improvements are gradual, and movements are more consistent.

So after you have figured out the desired goal and how to get to it, you learn to perfect it. You become fluent with the *what* and *how*. In this phase, aesthetics also come into play: how to make it your own, what is beautiful to you, and what is ugly, through your eyes. This part may take a little longer to go through. Gender differences can also affect the result of the goal in this phase. This is because of the physical makeup differences between the male and female. Female musicians tend to have smaller hands than their male counterparts; therefore, they might not have as vast of a reach on an instrument. For example, holding a tenth cord on the piano might pose a problem to most. However, female musicians have a wider vocal span or range than their male counterparts.

Next, you have the autonomous phase. This part takes months or years to get to. This is the part where you do whatever you've learned without thinking about it. It's automatic.

As its name suggests, it is "autonomous." This is months of practice and repetition, sometimes even years of doing the same thing over and over. A perfect example of this is walking. There was a study done in the Academy of Finland, where they found out how your brain responds to music. A team made up of people from Finland, England, and Denmark came together to study the response that music evokes in the brain, and after listening to a variety of music that included classical, jazz, and pop and focusing on timbre, rhythm, and tonality, they realized that music activates the auditory, motor, and limbic region in the brain. More interestingly, parts of the brain that are used for self-referential appraisal and aesthetic judgments were also affected by music. When lyrics are applied to music, the brain shifts the processing of musical features toward the right auditory cortex to better process the lyrics.

So, this is why I believe the human being's holistic makeup is wired for music. Every single sensory organ that exists in a human contributes to the transferring of music to the individual. You can read music. You can see music. You can hear music. You can feel music. One perfect example of this is Stevie Wonder. Stevie Wonder was blind from being in an oxygen incubator too long after a premature birth. The beautiful thing about his story is he played multiple instruments. And with his challenge of not seeing, he had to feel his way for all the different types of instruments that he played. The piano, drums, and harmonica are a few of the instruments he plays.

And the tricky thing about this is all of these instruments have different techniques to play them, and he had to feel his way through each one of them.

On another note, there are studies being conducted on how the deaf and the hard of hearing feel about and react to music. Some time ago, WebMD posted an article about a study being done by Dean Shibata, a medical doctor from the University of Rochester Medical Center in New York, on the relationship between music and deaf people titled "Deaf People Can Feel Music." In the study, he had ten deaf individuals who had experienced hearing loss from birth and eleven individuals who had normal hearing function. They were asked to let researchers know when they were able to detect a vibrating pipe in their hand. While vibrations were being transferred to the pipes, their brains were being scanned to pick up signals that were being transmitted to them.

Dr. Shibata and his team came to the realization that deaf people were able to identify vibrations in the same area of the brain that others use for hearing. Dr. Shibata's study also suggests that when deaf people are "feeling" the music, the experience could be the same as or similar to that of an individual who has normal hearing functions. This could explain how Heather Whitestone, who in 1995 became the first deaf individual to win the Miss America pageant, was able to dance so gracefully across the stage. My guess is she was able to feel the rhythm and bass and move and glide with them.

The World Innovation Summit for Education (WISE)

uploaded a project called "Feel the Music," by the Mahler Chamber Orchestra, which shows them inviting a group of deaf kids to be a part of the orchestra world. The kids were given the opportunity to conduct, touch the instruments, and sit within the orchestra to feel the vibrations from the instruments and also to interact with the musicians. The project goal was to allow the deaf individuals to sense the sound with their whole body and to interpret the feelings received. The kids did express in full how they felt the buildup in a song and knew when there was an intense part being played. They also related to the bass and drums, feeling the vibrations that were transmitted.

Another example is the composer known as Beethoven, a famous Western classical pianist who composed hundreds of pieces and became hard of hearing in his twenties and later on fully deaf. This setback had a major influence on the way he composed his music. The truth is no one really knows where music originated from. But based on what I've seen and my experiences, I am totally convinced that it came from God. Also, there is nothing you can do to stop music from entering your being. Like water, which can be found in almost anything that exists, music can also be found in almost anything. But I would take it a step further because unlike water, which can be cut off, channeled, and contained, music cannot be controlled in these ways. You can't stifle it, stop it, or prevent it. It will seep into the smallest crevices and air pockets. Nothing can go untouched by music, and therefore, music is more.

Chapter 2

The Fear within the Musician

We musicians have long nights and long days. At night, we are often playing out or just playing and practicing whatever comes to mind, or we go out to listen to music, to be inspired, and to be refreshed with ideas. There are two main reasons why we keep going as musicians, why we push through the struggle and the pain when we are told it won't work, the music won't make you any money, or you're not good enough. First, we do it because we can't help it. It is a part of our core, and it can't be separated from us. It is a dominant inner force that never stops reminding us about the music within. Second, we have our fears—fear of losing, fear of being second. The fear kills the dream inside. To be honest, the fear can be anything, but whatever that fear is, it keeps us going.

The most common fear that I've come across and that I've struggled with from time to time is self-doubt—worrying and wondering if I can play the piece the way it needs to be played, battling in my mind whether they would like the work that I have worked so hard to present. It's extremely draining mentally and can cripple any artist if he or she is not strong enough to encourage him- or herself to keep going in spite of what he or she might come across. Everything we do comes from a place deep within us, and we are fully aware that the road we walk is not one that supplies a necessity to life, even though it is essential to life. We do not work on spaceships, so we are far from being a rocket scientist. We do not create medicine where we heal people through tablets, so we are far from being doctors. We are not mathematicians or tech gurus with a new invention that will change the way we do things now. This means if it should come to a point where a decision has to be made between the arts and something else, then nine out of ten times, we will be the first to get the boot. We think about it all the time.

We see it all around us. Schools are cutting the arts programs left, right, and center. If a new church building project is taking place, and we have to make cuts to save money, the music department is cut first. We are always the first considered to go. This is how it's been, and having lots of money and being famous will not change anything. Knowing that this false security exists in music is quite troublesome, like a fly you can't kill. There are a lot of musicians out there who have it all and are still depressed. So, money won't change it. Because after the lights have been turned off and after everyone has gone home, you're the one who is left with your mind. And that's where the real battle lies. It plagues us, and we struggle with it. I'm not sure if this will ever go away. Even in the later stages of life, it will be present. The best thing I can do is recommend managing it the wisest way possible.

For those of us who only do music as a living, we eat and sleep music. We look to do nothing else but to play music. It is not because we can't fit into society but because we know there is a pull that calls us to walk a different path. Some paths are longer than others, and we understand and accept that. For some of us, our fears hit us when we step on stage. The lights and cameras, the noise or the silence, can be overwhelming to the point where we can't function. I remember those days when I used to freeze up knowing that I had a performance or that I had to do something in front of a large body of people. I never knew how to overcome it then, and as a result, I've had moments that were horrible because of my fear. And then for some, the fear hits us when everyone and everything is gone.

We know we all can't be the best. There will always be someone who plays better. Wow, to know and to accept this reality is such a hard task. Not only does it play on our minds, but if we are not careful, we could stop being creative. Can you sit for a moment and imagine yourself creating a song, a melody, a body of work, and another person comes in and does it better than you, the originator? These are the kinds of mental issues we deal with on a daily basis. Have you ever heard the song "I Will Always Love You" sung by Whitney Houston? Many of us know her just because of that song. I think we can all agree it helped catapult her career forward. What a lot of musicians don't know is that Whitney is not the original creator. Dolly Parton is. And she wrote the song over a separation between herself and her friend. It was originally a country and western song. But when it was added to *The Bodyguard* soundtrack, it became a hit for Whitney, and she was known by that song. Now, I'm fully aware that there are individuals who are gifted with the ability to write lyrics but might be lacking on the musical side to produce it or might not have the fame or following to get the music or their literature to the place they need it to be. Heck, there is a whole niche for it now in music that has turned into a market for those who can write behind the scenes without being recognized for it. It can be very profitable if they succeed in it. It's called "ghostwriting."

A ghostwriter is someone who is paid to write for another individual and gets no credit for the work that is done. Ghostwriting has been around for years; it is nothing new. The practice dates back to the fifth century BC. Scribes would produce work for politicians and royalty when they wanted to beef up their speech or if they lacked the intelligence to produce a body of work to get it to a certain orthodox point. If you don't believe me, you can ask George Washington. People might think he wrote his farewell speech, but in truth, he did not. He gave that responsibility to a guy named Alexander Hamilton. The practice once held a certain level of secrecy within the writing world, but in today's generation, it has become a very lucrative and profitable solution for many writers. Politicians, sports stars, music icons, and world leaders all have something in common that allows this niche to be so prosperous, and that is a lack of time. It is one of the main reasons for this niche. People don't have the time to do the work it requires so they hire someone to do it for them.

The foundation has grown so widespread with a variety of projects that you can get a ghostwriter for almost anything. Though it is in high demand, there is still a negative stigma to having a ghostwriter, especially in music. In the rap world, people who have been accused of having a ghostwriter have come under heavy scrutiny for it. In the music world, individuals want to know that the music that they listen to on a day-to-day basis can be attached to a face. People feel a sense of connection when they know the musician is writing his or her music and not someone else. If it should come out that the musician had to hire someone to do the music, he or she could be looked at as lying about what the music is saying. So that is just another thing that could scare a musician, but I'm not focusing on that. I'm talking about individuals who play and write their own stuff and it didn't take off the way they would have liked. Then, another person comes and uses their song, and it's like it was the borrower's song.

It's a hard thing to swallow at times, to know you will be second place in your own creation. The possibility of someone else taking what you've done and making it their own would drive any artist crazy, especially if he or she is not mentally secure with him- or herself. It is so important as an individual that you are strong mentally. If you are not, you can lose yourself. Yet we still go on because we love it, and we can't help it. I believe one thing that helps us a lot is if we can make good music or art, then it's worth it. We all have to understand these issues are not new. It's been happening since way before us. You can see it in our history of literature and music. To be quite honest, some of us fear not doing the music justice more than death itself. But if we learn how to manage these issues, then we can help encourage ourselves and others to keep moving forward. There have been many cases where musicians have given up because of the lack of money, or they have replaced the music with a responsibility that they have given more value to, like a family. But what most people don't know is the internal conflict that comes with those kinds of decisions—thinking back and wondering, *What if I continued?* You wonder how good you could have been if you had never met your girlfriend or boyfriend. Or seeing your son or daughter play more skillfully than you ever have, you wish you were the best at your skills to be the one to show your son or daughter how to play and to pass on the mantle. And the sad part is most musicians cry on the inside because they are conflicted with their emotions about these kinds of decisions.

Now I don't know about you, but for me, my music will always be a pillar of my foundation. To put a greater value to something that overshadows my music is me telling myself it's no longer a priority. What I cannot understand is back in the day, it used to be that the fathers of the house were known by, one, their names, and, two, their trades. The forefathers would set the tone for the business of the household, and the kids would most likely be the ones to take over the business and carry on the name and the trade. Who that son or daughter might become was determined by the fathers and forefathers. And we still can see some examples even in today's generation because some in the Jewish community still practice that life-style to this very day. But for us musicians, sometimes people want us to change who we are in order to suit the situation at hand. We are the ones who have the control as individuals to make changes to our situation. There are many musicians right now who go to bed angry, miserable, and full of regret because they change who they are to suit the situation that they are in, whether they are married or single. We still feel the effects of the decisions we made. The fact of the matter is there are individuals who do not play an instrument who believe that being a musician is a hobby. There are people out there who honestly think you cannot make a career out of it, and despite all the successful musicians out there now, they still think that it should not be so. It's something like being a very rich and successful black man and still being looked at as just being black. Then there are those who believe music is a dying art or that the support that once held the art as an important part of our culture is no longer there, so it will eventually die out.

At one point, it was mandatory in schools to learn an instrument. Now they've cut the music program so much that it has become a norm to have schools without a music program. Whichever direction a musician takes, he or she considers how his or her music will be affected by the changes he or she will go through. Every type of extracurricular activity a musician does, he or she must consider the possibility of an injury occurring and the level of severity that could happen because a musician's ability to function is solely based on his or her physical ability to perform. Whether the musician is a drummer, a keyboard player, a guitarist, or a bass player, if he or she is not in good physical health, he or she will be incapable of being effective in his or her craft.

Another of our greatest fears is injuring the part of our body we use most to perform. Every musician who is in music culture always thinks about how much physical work he or she takes on, making sure that the work is not too taxing on the area of his or her musicianship. The goal will always be to protect the hands, feet, or voice. Every musician can testify that the thought of losing the ability to play sends chills down our backs. This is why we don't accept certain jobs. For example, I could never see myself doing a construction job, lifting and pulling every single day for eight to twelve hours. Every job has its own issues that come with it. There's no way you would go into construction with the mind-set of you not getting a cut or scrape here and there or you bucking your toe into something or something falling on your feet. There are just too many possibilities for musicians to hurt their hands or feet in that field. So, we usually stay in fields that would put us far from danger if the choice is there. Obviously, this does not apply to every musician because we have different goals and desires.

For example, the army has their own band, and it is made up of extremely talented and well-trained musicians. But the musicians are in the army, and they have to do physical training to meet certain requirements. They play for a living, but because it's the army, they still have to be in shape, which requires them to do what soldiers do. Personally speaking, I believe that most times, people do not understand us as musicians. They don't get it. They think we are weird, nerds. People think we caused the downfall of multiple generations, or we helped. They think we are players, and we don't contribute anything to society. And it plays on our fears because we are people too, and we feel and hurt. Being prejudged before even knowing who we are as individuals has put us in a place where we have no choice but to lock ourselves away in our minds and hearts.

I was once denied being with someone because I was a

musician. The person's parent said, "You won't make any money doing that." Her daughter was studying to become a nurse, and the parent felt her daughter needed someone to match her status.

Now, I must say that everything that I have discussed in this chapter has one stem that connects all of the issues together. And this stem is called *insecurity*. As individuals, every one of us deals with insecurity on some level. Whether we deal with it on a higher scale or deal with it at a minimum level, we all come across it in one way or another. One might ask, "Is it healthy to have a little insecurity?" I believe so. It helps with character building. How you manage and deal with your feelings pertaining to issues that you might be going through will also determine how strong your inner man and your emotional state will be the next time an issue should arise.

Even your livelihood can allow insecurities to arise within you. If the economy takes a turn for the worse and you start to wonder whether your job will be affected, it could cause you to worry and become insecure. And with issues that play on your insecurity, you then start to question yourself, wondering, *Am I doing what I need to do? Am I going to be okay? Will I be successful?*

If your son should say you're a horrible father or your girlfriend said, "I hate you; you're a horrible boyfriend," or your parents looked at you differently based on how you handled different opportunities in the past, all these examples could play on your insecurity. There are many avenues to insecurity that we might not be aware of. There is a term *inferiority complex*, which describes a behavioral tendency known as "striving for superiority." This, in a nutshell, means that you step on the feelings of the people around you. Individuals with an inferiority complex make people feel smaller in order to make themselves feel bigger. This behavior shows that there are insecurities in the individual who is acting this way. Being afraid is nothing new. Everyone has a little fear inside. How you manage that fear will either put you in a place to conquer it or allow it to conquer you.

According to dictionary.com, fear is a distressing emotion aroused by impending danger. Yes, we know there are different types of fear, like homophobia, acrophobia, and ":testophobia," but every great king or queen, ruler, conqueror, or fighter will tell you it serves a bigger purpose than just getting you to run or freeze up and cower in silence. Fear is also a good thing. Fear keeps you focused. It keeps you grounded. It keeps you from making reckless decisions. Every one of us has had that moment where we chose not to do that "musical thing" because of fear, and maybe it was the fear that caused us to not crash and burn, or maybe it made the whole team have a great show. Some of us create multiple alter egos to distribute different behavioral patterns to or to get away from something or someone. For example, Beyoncé will speak about "Sasha Fierce" every so often, and when she does, she talks about how fearful or timid she is compared to "Sasha Fierce," who is bold and outspoken. Fear tends to have a negative connotation to it, but one thing I will say is that fear keeps your perspective in check.

Chapter 3

Drugs

C oke, weed, alcohol, and crack have been and will continue to be a part of entertainment. No matter what type of genre, you will find it in every part of music and every part of entertainment. It has crept in and solidified itself as a part of the industry. At times, I wonder if it's an element that is fueling entertainment. I really do not know for a fact, but I do know it goes hand in hand with it. At almost every secular studio session that I've done, they would ask if I would like some weed, or I would have to work in the midst of it because it's just what they do as musicians and entertainers. When you are about to record or lay a track down, if your body is tense, the first thing they will do is give you some strong alcohol to help cool your nerve and help you relax. And I see why they would use it to aid in helping them to achieve a desired goal.

I remember going to a big house out on Long Island owned by a major artist whom I cannot mention. He had turned the house into a studio, and I met up with a friend there to lay something down for him. Upon entering the house, you came to the stairway. One side went up and the other down. On the main floor was where they had the offices and regular business transactions. They brought me to the waiting area, and they had alcohol and weed in the room. It was just there chilling. No one was smoking it at the moment, but it was just there. Now I was never the one to smoke even though I was around it my whole life. But before I would reach for a cigar or weed, I would most likely take a drink. This showed me and opened my eyes to the normality of the music world. You will not find one without the other. And if you are not secure in who you are, you can get swept away by the people and the hype that come with it.

Smoking was just not for me. I can remember moments when I was asked to play for a church with random musicians. And every so often, we would meet up after the show and just talk, crack jokes, and chill. But for every opportunity like that, every so often, one individual would have a cigar, some weed, or liquor, and he or she would smoke or drink it right after the church or club or whatever event that they were playing at.

Billie Holiday, a renowned jazz singer, had a tough life. She came from small beginnings and was not shy about being a little raw in her music. Billie was born on April 7, 1915, and was raised by her mom. Billie went into prostitution after she left her mom and supported herself on the streets for three years before being locked up. After she came out of prison, she attempted to get a job at a nightclub as a dancer, where she failed, but then she told the club owner she could also sing. When she opened her mouth and saw that they all stopped what they were doing, she realized that it was something she could do. Billie made a lot of memorable hits like "Strange Fruit," but despite all the noise she was creating in the music industry, her negative habits put a darkness over the light she had. Billie was known to be a heavy drinker and was introduced to heroin by her first husband, another musician, a trombonist by the name of Jimmy Monroe.

Now, the sad part about this was the money she started to make on the road went into supporting her habits. It became a downward spiral for her. The reason I brought this up is because you would assume that she would use the money to help fix the issues, but it was the opposite. The money was aiding the issues. In the end, it cost her a price she didn't have to pay. I would like to bring your attention to a few points that I think support the platform for drugs. The environment, the fame and wealth, the supplier and the buyer, and peer pressure.

Their Surroundings

Yes, it is true the musician spends a lot of time on the road. A working musician is not necessarily limited to only nights; he or she works through the day if he or she is connected and really good at what he or she does. But the truth of the matter is we mostly work at nights, and the environment in which we work supports a healthy ground to drink and get wasted, to get drunk and to get high. Now this is not limited to the night scene only, but it often occurs at night. Because they have the alcohol and drugs in clubs, bars, studios, and private events.

Now it is only natural that a musician will run into drugs and alcohol because the environment in which we work is laced with them. Look at all the jazz bars, nightclubs, and open mic spots. What does every one of these locations have in common? Yup, you got it—it's alcohol. I myself have played at locations where the bartender would just send liquor my way just because. Maybe he was having a good time, or maybe I was doing an excellent job. Maybe he had a strong crowd because there was live music. Who knows? But what I did realize was I got a consistent flow of alcohol my way. And it wasn't to say that he was trying to get me drunk because if you can't play, then you can't work, but I think it's like a relationship in the sense that they know we help each other in a "screw sense." What I really want for us to understand is that this is not only attached to a fixed location. When we travel privately on our tour busses or by car, that environment, though it may be small, can still be set up to help the flow of drugs and alcohol.

The Fame and Wealth

As you climb the ladder of fame and wealth as a musician, you will quickly realize how your position and money can either help to stop your bad habits or help to transform them into bigger monsters than they are. And just as how fame and wealth affect our quality of life, well, they also affect the quality of drugs and alcohol. The drugs tend to be a lot more expensive. The drugs are purer, and the alcohol is stronger. Everything upgrades at this phase in your life, and therefore, the possibilities of the negative habits becoming demons are that much greater if the individual is not prepared to show restraint and discipline. I must stress everyone under the umbrella of the entertainment world also has to cross this road in one way or the other.

Fame, on another note, has its side effects also. There is a level of transparency that you have to be comfortable with in order for you to manage and get through in one piece. The lack of privacy might be a new issue that you have to deal with if you're not okay with being an open book to be read twenty-four/seven. Then there is the bar or standard that the public expects you to live by. You find yourself trying to be perfect in their eyes, trying to do what is right, trying to keep up with the trend, trying to show that you're a role model. Gaining the tools and the momentum to keep up with their demands can be a real issue. And then there are the haters who hate on you just because you've reached a place where you've never been before. It's so ridiculous the reasons why someone would hate on you or scrutinize you. Can you imagine the amount of stress a person would be going through if he or she were dealing with all these factors at once? We then have to assume that all these are logical factors that could cause any individual to drink, smoke, or use drugs. The drugs now become a way of escape for most entertainers to help them deal with the pressure they experience on a daily basis, and as a result, functioning drug addicts are created.

The Dealer

For a dealer to be around musicians or high celebs, it's like a poor person hitting the lotto. Being around people in entertainment will surely put this individual on the map. He or she gets access to the musician's or celeb's inner circle, and his or her network will increase rapidly. Now compared to the average Joe, I do think the dealer would show favoritism to the entertainer or high-end client, either because the individual is wealthy or because of his or her status and connections. Therefore, you can only imagine that the dealer's best product would be at the buyer's leisure. What every person should understand is the dealer has a list or record of the purchases made. Some dealers are very professional and keep records of the time of purchase, location of purchase, and who is doing the buying. What people should seriously consider is that if a record is being kept, then it opens the door to other issues that may arise in the future, like blackmail or being exposed to the public at the dealer's discretion.

Drug dealers are human beings also, which means they are susceptible to greed, jealousy, anger, and the lure of fame. It's now a big thing for dealers to anonymously give up their clients to public sources for whatever reason they might have. Dealers are turning their clients into an "arsenal." They can do damage to the client's reputation or use him or her as an example to prove a point. This should be a wake-up call to everyone that there is no loyalty between the client and dealer, and they should understand that a dealer can turn on anyone at any time. How do I know this is so?

Radar (radaronline.com) made a post entitled "Celebrity Drug Dealer Tells All—Who's Hooked, Who's Recovered and Who'll Die Next." They talk about all the information that was brought to them by the drug dealers themselves. There were over twenty high celebrity individuals mentioned on the list. The drug dealers turned in information about specific clients they had provided with drugs.

We as entertainers need to be more careful about the choices we make and how they will affect us long term. Dealers are less emotional and more careless with the client's information, and they could be willing to give up information for the right price.

The Consumer

As we know, we are in the age of technology. The internet right now acts as a master portal to different things you may desire. And the youths have taken ownership of the keys to the doorways. There have been so many young millionaires who have been born from the internet, and as time passes, the millionaires are getting younger and younger, it seems. Celebs like Chris Brown and Justin Bieber who got their break pretty young are examples of that. Being hot and young are excellent attributes in the music business. If you start out young, there is a good chance of you becoming a megastar if you can keep up with what it takes. But with being young also comes the young mind-set, the lack of responsibility, temper tantrums, and immature decisions that are made. There is no doubt that a young millionaire is going to buy any and everything he or she desires. It is expected, especially if he or she is coming from humble beginnings. Also, the opportunity to try new things and to have new experiences will also be at his or her leisure. Young people with millions to blow tend to get caught up with the party scene. And once you start to get caught up in the party scene, you make friends and begin going to clubs. With clubs come alcohol and drugs. It happens all the time. If you don't believe me, you can take a look at Lindsey

Lohan and Charlie Sheen, and you will have an idea of what I'm talking about.

Now I do see it as a trend. I'm not sure if it's going to be a socially acceptable thing to do, but for now, it's trending. I mean even in schools where we hang out and meet up, we have weed candy, weed brownies, and weed cake. It's everywhere. Even teachers smoke and drink on their personal time because you have to remember that they are musicians first before anything. But not all musicians are down with it. Some musicians stay away from it because of their beliefs or their religion, or they just don't let it affect them, but these individuals are still fewer in number compared to the many who are doing drugs. If you don't believe me, check the jazz lounge and the nightclub. With the big music players who teach by day as a profession and entertain by night, you will see exactly what I'm talking about. And this is why I think it's a socially accepted behavior in the music world. But though it may be socially acceptable, the dark side to this vastly outweighs the good side. We are losing so many great musicians to drugs. When the musical workload becomes hard, then we tend to be dependent on the weed, coke, and alcohol to get us through the situation.

This is why I say it is very important for us as musicians to be psychologically and mentally strong for the different types of issues we might come across. We don't only work on ways to make connections to meet people and to network but to help prepare our minds for the different twists and turns that await us down the road. It is so sad that no one is accountable and teaching our musicians how to go about walking this path when the different issues arise. So many musicians lose themselves while being on tour to the use of drugs. So many of us die in our backyard because no one cared since we are musicians. Do I think it's a problem? Yes, and an extreme one at that. Do I think it needs to be addressed and managed? Yes. But the quicker we understand that this is a problem, the quicker we can come up with strategic measures to help ensure the health and safety of the individuals.

Peer Pressure

Being famous or known for any particular thing gives one a cool feeling. Everyone loves the feeling of being the man, the go-to guy, the one everyone looks to for answers, of being connected to people who are important and having a certain level of authority. Sometimes in order to get into the "clique" or to join a particular group, you have to hang like them and party like them, or you won't be accepted. Most musicians don't realize this until it's too late. We try so hard at times to fit in that we forget our standards in the process just so we can get attention from people. In some music scenes, it is cool to do weed and drugs. And there will be times when the individual could be looked down on if he or she refuses to smoke or do drugs with the crew and thus is excluded from the group.

The word *peer* refers to a person who is of equal standing, whether by age or status. Usually, adolescents are influenced by the group based on the need to be down with them. If the group values a particular kind of behavior, then the person coming into the group will feel some type of pressure to conform to the way things are done within the group. This is looked at as a "peer group." As individuals get older, peer pressure becomes less influential, but it can still have an effect on the individual's behavior. One thing that I have learned is that people are not always pressured by a group or an individual. No one person is the same. And thus, every person learns in a different way.

One way pressure can present is visual. The joy and the reaction that one sees in another party or individual can be a form of pressure. We see the money and the luxury lifestyle of the rich and famous, and it can be a temptation to emulate their behavioral pattern to feel the joy they are feeling.

Why do you think the industry put so much money into music videos and movies? They show what they do to entice the viewer. So, if a person sees someone getting enjoyment from drinking or doing drugs, that individual might be curious to see if he or she can experience the same joy. It's a form of social learning. Social learning is extremely imperative and a necessary phase for our survival as human beings. But if not managed correctly, if the information being received is amiss, it can become self-destructive. But just as we can learn the bad, we can also learn how to unlearn the bad with social learning.

Drugs are any substance, with the exception of food and water, that when inhaled or taken into the body, alter the body's functions, either physically or psychologically. Drugs are a problem. And it needs to be handled, or we will continue to lose great musicians to it.

Drugs react in the brain to change how the body feels. Seeing that the brain is the control center for the body, a message is sent to the rest of the body based on information received from chemical messengers or drugs. Chemical messengers are made in the body to do a specific job in the brain. But drugs are chemical messengers that were made outside the body and as a result can send wrong signals to the body, creating problems—for example, seeing and hearing things that are not real or feeling things that are not there. Drugs can increase your heart rate, make your pupils bigger, and slow your body down. They can also affect the way you eat, see, hear, move, smell, and think. Now in some cases, if you have been taking drugs for a long time, you will start to develop what is called "tolerance," which means you are getting used to being on the drug. Most times, people see it as a good thing, where they feel they are above it or can handle it, or because they don't feel like it's doing anything to them, they can stop anytime they want. But what people fail to realize is that rising tolerance levels mean that the individual is killing the part of the body that is responsible for resisting the drug.

Now at this stage, you will want the "high" that you crave, and in order to get it, you will have to do stronger drugs. Also, it will start to become more expensive to maintain the habit, and it will get ugly quickly. Some drugs may alter your physical appearance. Drugs like crystal meth and amphetamines cause you not to be hungry; hence you become very thin, weak, and unhealthy. Many of these drugs cause liver damage, or limit your body's ability to fight off infections. Stroke, heart problems, and your body temperature being altered up and down can lead to death. Here are a few drugs that are commonly used among entertainers:

- heroin—an opioid drug synthesized from morphine
- cocaine—a powerful and potent brain stimulant
- marijuana—dry leaves, flowers, and stems from the *Cannabis sativa* plant
- meth—a stimulant drug
- ecstasy—a psychedelic stimulant drug
- speed—stimulant drugs
- stimulants—a group of drugs that cause an increase in attention and energy and the blood pressure to elevate

Chapter 4

Dating a Musician

emales, females, females. I have had my share of females. Black, White, Hispanic, fat, skinny, and so on, you name it. But this was not always so. When I was young, I never had a girlfriend. Growing up in Jamaica, I was always the third wheel, always hoping to have the girl I had the biggest crush on. But in truth, I was never seen as boyfriend material. I was the one who was called "the advice giver." In other words, I was only good enough to give wisdom. The school I used to attend was called Excelsior. And Excelsior stemmed from the kindergarten to the primary to the high school and the college level.

My first few experiences with girls happened when I

started in the primary school. I can remember to this very day being in first grade trying to be a part of the group, but I could never fit in. It was quite the experience, I must, say because I could not intellectually or socially decode how I should feel when it came to girls. Maybe it was my quirky behavior or my nerdy look that would make them stay away from me. Who knows? But it was something that I thought about for a long time. Even in high school, I was known for my talent, but as a regular person, I was never seeing as the likable one to be in a relationship with. But yet they liked my playing.

When I came to the United States, I had to go through high school all over again. But there was a difference this time around. Girls actually started to like me. It was a switch I could not explain. I didn't change my behavior or mannerisms, so the only thing that could have caused this to happen was my environment—at least that was what I thought. And at this time, I started to play the piano a lot more. I wasn't that skilled yet, but I was known for it. Now there was a moment in my life where it clicked for me.

My first girlfriend was a person I met from a church gig I used to play for in Brooklyn. My cousin, who played for different churches, took a (nine-to-five) job, and there were time conflicts with his new schedule. So, as a result, he called me up and asked whether I wanted to take his position and make some money while doing what I loved. And I jumped at it. It was because of my music that I got my first girlfriend. Now, why was this significant to me? Because it was at that time, I really decided to take my playing seriously. I made a conscious decision to be committed to the music wholeheartedly. I was practicing for hours and learning as much as I could at that time. And I realized, not only did my practicing raise the level of my skills, but it drew a whole bunch of girls to me. And it put my thought processing on a whole different level. People are automatically attracted to people with talent. If a person that you knew would not give you the time of day, should he or she ever become aware of how influential you are with your music, you do not even have to approach that person. She or he will come to you, especially if you are on your game. It's just something that happens. Any musician will tell you that this is real. Not only that, but your skill can determine the level of people who are attracted to you. Now mind you, if you are weird and don't act in a way that is pleasing to the opposite sex, you still will have issues getting someone. That is a given. Now some individuals might not want to be with you long term. But they will be with you for a little while just so that they can be associated with you. These individuals are not gold diggers. I call them "hitchhikers," and this is why.

A musician can have the best skill with his or her instrument and still be broke. And we see that every day. But if you pay attention to that same musician in some cases, he or she will have someone who is hot in every way, in looks and in physique. And within a year's time, that same musician will have a different person. Now this varies from person to person based on his or her beliefs, ideology, and social situation. I can say it is extremely hard for us as musicians to decipher other people's intentions while dating.

There was a time when I was questioning my exes about whether they were with me for my talent or for me. And I know musicians go through this at times, some more than others. Now I must admit that it's the male or the female musician who sometimes acts up in the relationship and calls it off. We can be emotional. Yes, our feelings may fluctuate at times, but we are easily calmed by good music. But if we are honest, both parties share the responsibility. And in order to address the issue, we have to talk to both the males and the females. There are females out there who have a lot of male partners, and there are males who have a lot of female partners. It's on both ends. But this is not always the case, because there are musicians out there who are truly looking for that special someone. But even those musicians get a few experiences before they find that right person.

My interaction with females took off after high school. I was playing at a "nice level" and was traveling with different groups and choirs, and it put me in a place where I was accessible to all kinds of women.

I knew of male and female musicians who were very open about their relationships.

Female "A" was a good friend of my girlfriend's, who had dark skin and was slim and pretty. She could sing. He met her after high school, and around this time, he was playing in the Seventh Day Circle in Brooklyn. She was extremely shy, but like I said, once he could play, he did not need to approach any females. There was a look he said that he gave her, and when she saw him, she knew what that look meant. She eventually went over to him, and he started to talk. Then they started to meet up—breakfast dates, brunch, dinners—and before you knew it, they were all over each other.

My friend and I would talk about girls a lot. We would compare stories on how we got them and what our experience would be like. I will never forget the time he told me about when "Female A" told him one of the reasons she came over was because she couldn't help but think about the way he played, and she would, in her mind, substitute him playing the piano for him playing on her—you know, him running his fingers all over her body. Hey, I mean, it was funny at the time, and we cracked up about it. These are the moments we as musicians will treasure for life—the little subtle experience that makes us secretly chuckle within the confined space of our hearts. For most of my musical friends, it is similar. Most male musicians were single for a minute before they settled down because they enjoyed the life of just having no strings attached. And when I mean single, I mean they might have been in relationships but nothing serious. He did it for little while, but I was never about that life. It wasn't for me.

"Female B," a friend of mine, met her boyfriend in college. She decided to study music in school, and as a result, her skills began to sharpen. As her skills begin to mature, the cali-ber of males changed. Not only could she get the males who pretended like she was below them, but she could now have the males who were just as skillful or even prettier and more intelligent than she was. "Male B" was Spanish, either Puerto Rican or Dominican. She stated she was practicing in one of the practice rooms at her school, and he heard her playing. He stood outside for some time, but he didn't notice that she saw him. She began to show off a little to make him want to stay, and it worked. He then knocked on her door and asked if he could sit in and listen to her. You might be saying, "Some luck, huh?" Nope. That was what she wanted to happen, and it did. She was feeling herself so hard, no one could take her off cloud nine.

After she went through her practice, he began to compliment her on how beautifully she played. She sat and listened to him speak. But in her head she was thinking she was going to have this young man as her man. So, he began to tell her that he was a singer and had always wanted to learn the piano, but he never got around to it. Then he said the four magical words that get every musician going: *Can you teach me?* Now let me say this. It's only magical when it's a person you know you want, and there is no effort—and I mean absolutely no effort—needed on your part to make it happen. That is what makes it magical. She was with him for a while, but she broke it off because of whatever reason. She didn't say what it was.

Now the reason for me giving you these two examples here is because there is a negative stigma that musicians are dogs. To be quite frank, relationships are just as good or bad whether you're a musician or not. The thing that makes musicians look bad is that we have to work with other individuals who work in entertainment, and people assume that in this field, it's all about sleeping with each other. The media also should share the responsibility of causing insecurity in individuals who date musicians because they paint this idea using pictures and music videos with men surrounded by women or women surrounded by male figures to promote a certain lifestyle. If you should ask any working musician, he or she will tell you that what the media promotes is a highly exaggerated idea.

There was a study done on men when it comes to buying a car. The study showed that a car by itself that's being advertised has significantly less of a chance of being sold compared to a car that has a beautiful woman placed beside it. But does this mean that every car dealer has a woman perched up at their dealership? No. The first thing people, female or male, should understand when it comes to dating a musician who is doing music full-time or part-time is they have to be secure with who they are in the relationship. Because it will be tested by the "Nos" they will hear, and the many examples of "I have rehearsal or gig so I can't make it" that come along with it. You will have to accept his or her world, and you will need to understand the way the musician lives in that world. You might not be first all the time either.

As you date a musician, you will see that the music is his or her baby. It's a piece of him- or herself. That is the number-one priority. It does not mean you will be in last place, but you have to come into the relationship knowing that the value that is placed on the music will be extremely high, and if you're not careful, it could shake the foundation of the relationship. A musician is always on the grind trying to get hired for that next event, trying to put him- or herself out there with his or her music to be seen and recognized. And at times, it will cost the relationship money and time. Yes, date nights will be limited, and time hanging out might be limited based on his or her musical schedule. Also, most musicians spend a lot of money on equipment—a lot of money! So, in most cases, they might not want to go out because funds might be a little low, and they do not want to be embarrassed by not being able to pay for their meal or to treat their significant other. Also, a lot of musicians get paid cash. And sometimes they don't get all the funds that were agreed upon based on how profitable the show was when the contractor is doing some shady thing and isn't willing to pay. Hence, they may be short with funds.

Would you be willing to step into a musician's world knowing all of this will take place? Because it is a tough journey with a lot of hills. Musicians find inspiration from anything. They will at times drop every single thing that they are doing just so that they can save or record a melody, an idea, or a phrase. And during this time, they are usually constructing music in their heads. They might become unresponsive if they are on to something. But it's also that time when they are a little vulnerable because when something new is being created, it automatically becomes their baby. You will need to be their encourager and their number-one fan with their music. At times, they might write a song about their very own relationship or about that significant other. Will you be okay with that? Because, like I said, inspiration comes from anything for musicians—the good, the bad, and the ugly. They will turn anything into music or a song. Then you will have the long nights being awake listening to music.

There have been times when I have listened to a melodic phrase over and over and over again. Even though it was ten seconds long, I ended up listening to it for a half an hour to an hour, just trying to learn and play it perfectly. It was so bad my mom, who heard me stopping the song and rewinding it back to the top of the phrase over and over and over again, came to me and begged me to let the song continue playing because she couldn't take it anymore.

Being with a musician will annoy the hell out of you, especially if you're not into music like that. We can sit and listen to one song for a whole day, and we will listen like it's the first time every time. Going to shows with musicians can be tiresome or have you worn out because of lack of sleep, which most musicians who have two jobs will agree is extremely hard, especially if you have work the following day. And they usually will be the first ones to be at their show and the last ones to leave. The after-show talks with random individuals and their bandmates about how crazy that solo was and how the crowd responded to the presentation could seem to last forever to someone who has no clue about what is going on. Random jokes and downtime are necessary for the musician to unwind and to get him or her to a place where he or she can be relaxed to pay full attention to a significant other. I cannot begin to stress how important it is.

There have been many times when my musician friends are so happy and free when they are playing, and by the end of the show, their mood changes because their significant other is upset because they might be taking a little long or they don't want to wait themselves. And they end up arguing and losing out on opportunities to get to really know the musician inside his or her element. The last thing any musician wants to hear about after any show is anything that will put a damper on his or her spirit. We don't want to hear about any family issues or the bad things that happened in the day. Especially if they had a show that went south, please do not choose that time to talk or to confront him or her about something that might have happened earlier or days before. It will not end well.

Timing is key. A musician is locked in with time. They go hand in hand. Every musician has an internal clock that is dominant within him or her. This is why we can be on beat regardless of what is happening around us. So please be sensitive when bringing up information.

Then we all know there will be groupies. As long as you work in the entertainment business, there will be groupies. There are all kinds of groupies: groupies for singers, band members, and actors. And people will hit on all of them. And you will need to accept that. Sometimes, a musician is not even paying any attention to it until someone else mentions it. Be careful. But I believe as long as he or she is not violating the relationship, then everything should be okay. It's going to take a lot from you because you will see inside the world of a musician, and it can become overwhelming. You will have to accept it. It's all a part of his or her world. You cannot change the world he or she is in, but you can change the response.

Trust will be a big factor in your relationship with a musician. Musicians may get the opportunity to go on tour, and if so, you will need to talk with them because it could break or make the relationship. Some musicians go away for a week, some for a month, and some for a six-month period. It goes according to the tour schedule. These are areas that will need in-depth discussion because being away from each other for a long period of time can cause issues to arise. Sometimes when individuals marry a musician, they are under the impression that the musician will not be a musician anymore. I could never understand why they want us to stop being a musician just because we are married. I had a friend who would practice at night after work, and his wife would tell him to stop practicing because she was not going to bed without him. It caused issues because he would continue to practice, and she would be upset because she would be up and would refuse to sleep without him being in bed.

Now it is so important we individuals understand who we really want to settle down with. I was taught when you get married issues like habits, debts, and finances, *everything*, gets multiplied either for the better or for the worse. If we truly love someone for who he or she is, we should always try to maximize each other's potential and try to strengthen the weak areas in our relationship.

My experiences with couples whose makeup includes a musician have shown me that the other individual often thinks the musician will not be playing his or her instrument anymore or as often, or he or she should not be going out and doing shows anymore because they are married. These people eventually want the musician to change from being a musician. This does not necessarily occur right away, but over a period of time. They don't want you to be doing so much music, or they don't want you to be as involved. Maybe the money is not being made right then, and the music scene is slow, so you have to get a nine-to-five job to make ends meet, or you have a kid and your time has to be given to other areas in your life. All of these changes that occur come with life itself. Does it mean you have to change who you are? No. You have to adapt to the situation and evolve. Now I do believe that situations will cause you to alter plans, but it doesn't mean you should stop being who you are. I do understand every musician won't be out there. And I understand only a few will be famous. But whether you are famous and playing across the whole world with millions watching you or you are just playing in your basement in front of your mirror, imagining you're at Carnegie Hall, being true to yourself and doing what you love must remain the number-one goal and path to true happiness in anyone's life.

Here are some pointers to remember if you are with a musician whether as a girlfriend or boyfriend or husband or wife.

- Make sure you are good and mentally prepared for this role. As the outside individual coming into his or her world, it's going to be to be extremely important you are rested, you don't feel stress about anything, and you cut down on the arguing before showtime as quickly and early as possible. All this affects his or her mind and could cause him or her not to perform to the best of his or her ability.

- A good way to help a musician function is if he or she is fully aware that you're okay, then he or she won't have to worry about you, which allows him or her to focus on his or her music. That helps everyone to be happy. A musician needs to be calm and in a positive state of mind to be effective in his or her music.

- You have to respect the band members. Whether you like them or not, most of your significant other's time is being spent with them. When he or she is not with you, he or she is with them. When he or she is on the road, he or she is with them. If a fight should happen while being on the road, most likely every band member will have each other's back, whether it is the person's fault or not.

- The relationship between band members is a very complex one. This bond may last for years. It's a bond that runs very deep and is forged through the good and the bad times. There is nothing more filling to a band than when they know they killed the show and nothing more humbling than when they are booed off stage. It is that high and low process that determines the level of the bond. It is very imperative that you understand the dynamics before speaking anything negative about the other band members. Do not think you can come between that. Do not think you can break it apart because you cannot. If a band separates, most of the time, it's an internal issue that could not be resolved.

- The band is also watching how you treat the band member you are with. A lot of times, individuals who are dating a musician don't realize that the band is paying close attention to the way their bandmate is being treated. There have been serious talks within the band about if the individual a bandmate is dating is in his or her best interest or if the relationship is a healthy one. Be extremely careful. Musicians do not only fight for their bandmates on a physical level but also on a mental level. We watch to see if the relationship interferes with the band's time and to see if the bandmate is slipping off his or her game. I've been a part of bands where we talked to a bandmate about leaving the relationship because it wasn't healthy for the individual.

It happens. It's a pity it doesn't happen often because it would save a lot of headache down the road. I wish we were more accountable for each other.

- You have to develop a thick skin. Musicians can be some of the most sarcastic individuals on the planet. Not only that, but they will joke on you for days, and I mean laugh and laugh and laugh and laugh. Most times, we see something, and it becomes a group topic while on stage. And we could be talking without moving our mouths, having a full-blown conversation, cracking jokes, and carrying on, and no one would even know.

  On another note, if the band is being playful with you, that is a way the band shows that they are comfortable with you. And your willingness to be a part of it and to just relax and let loose with the band also allows them to fight for you when you're not around. If the band does not trust you, they won't stand for you when you're not around.

- Also, if the band is famous and your significant other is a star, you will need to share him or her with the fans. There might be time when you are out and a fan will come up and ask for an autograph or a picture or just a shake of hand or a hug. It will be in your best interest to push your jealousy or emotions aside because this is a part of his or her world, and you signed up to be a part of it. Also, it is the fans who pay the bills, so suck it up and let it go. You are with the star regardless, so you will always have the exclusiveness to him or her.

Rivalry

Rivalry has been a part of society from before history even took shape. From the days of Cain and Abel to our current era, there has always been a desire to be the dominant player in the ring. I do believe that this is also the case when a musician who has been trained tends to feel like he or she has the upper hand over a musician who was born with the talent but has no training.

I grew up knowing that I would be a musician from the time I held two combs pretending that they were drumsticks. My first instrument was the drums, and I started to play at age six and matured over the years that passed. No one taught me how to play. I knew how to play, and my body knew what to do and how to achieve it. It is something that to this very day, I do not know how to explain. I would sit and watch drummers for hours and then go home and practice on my dresser, pretending it was a drum. Every lotion bottle, hair grease can, or facial product was a part of a drum that existed in my world.

Fast-forward into the future. I ended up meeting my first music teacher, whose name was Miss Grant. She taught the choir in Excelsior Primary. We would compete against different schools in the parish. We would beat everyone. And we still have the trophies to prove it. Miss Grant was extremely talented. She played an array of instruments and was very skilled. When I got to the school, she at once knew I was a musician. She gave me a conga drum and asked me to play it. Now anyone can say it's an easy instrument to play because you can just do anything, and it would sound like a beat. But at the time when I auditioned, I was seven, and the rhythm patterns and techniques I was showing were the patterns professionals were doing at that time. So, she decided to take me under her wing and showed me how to develop my skills with this type of instrument. I got so good at it that I received a scholarship to attend the Jamaica School of Music by the age of eleven. I studied drums for three years there.

I left the drums a long time ago, and there is a part of me deep inside that cries for them. But I put the drums down and picked up the piano, and I have never looked back. The thing about the piano is even though I was self-taught, I had a little help along the way. For the drums, it was natural, and I did everything myself until I got to school. The reason I talk about my experiences with the piano is because I was often looked down on because I wasn't trained, and I had nothing behind my name as far as a music school when I decided to play the piano. I cannot speak for anyone else, but my stay in New York City opened my eyes to how seriously the name of an institution can shape your musical career.

Now, though that might not have anything to do with how skillful you become, it does affect how much work you might get and the types of work you might get. I was always a church musician, so I never thought about playing full-time outside of church. From time to time, I would end up playing with different types of musicians from all over, and when I would come around someone who had been trained, I could hear it clear as day, the difference in their musical vocabulary. Even in speech, when they spoke about a chord or a change in chord progression, I would wonder at times what they were talking about.

Now I am fully aware that there are different styles of music, but for this purpose, we will look at only the basic genre that helped to shape Western music in the twenty-first century, which includes classical, jazz, gospel, rock, and so on.

Okay, for example, anyone who has taken the route to learn an instrument on his or her own will tell you the first system he or she might learn or come across is the number system. That's how most untrained musicians communicate: 12345678. Anyone can attest to this. And though both untrained and trained musicians know the system, there is still a different level in applying the number system that sets the trained apart from the untrained. There have been many times when I was the untrained person. When I started to play the piano, I could play any song in the key of C. I learned the number system and the scales, and my ears were so developed, if I heard it, I could play it. But there was one huge problem. It was the only key I could play in, which meant I could only play a keyboard with the transpose button in it. So, if a singer would modulate, then all I had to do was click the transpose button, and it would shift the note higher or lower, depending on if you clicked up or down.

Back then, there was no need to learn the other keys because of this feature, or so I thought. I thought it was the best thing since sliced bread. I held on to it without realizing how it was killing me faster than I was growing musically. Night after night, I stayed up, practicing all those different songs in one key, thinking I was the man because I was playing difficult songs and pulling them off. Yet I wasn't really playing them in their true key. It wasn't until a very embarrassing moment while I was playing a baby grand piano that my skills were exposed, showing how underdeveloped I was. And from that day, I decided to never use that transpose feature again. I've since been playing in every key.

So, every now and then, I would get the opportunity to play with the professionals, and they would call out numbers from time to time, but my application would always be different until one of the individuals from the group would show me how to apply what they were saying. I worked hard on learning how to apply it, but I saw myself not getting anywhere until a friend said to me I had to change the way I thought about music. I struggled a lot because of the way I thought music was supposed to be. But experience has taught me that for every melody and every song that is created, your mind-set has to adapt to that melody and that song.

Now every pianist knows that there are three octaves above middle C and three octaves of C below middle C.

The first thing I worked on in my musicianship was to shift my mind-set on how I looked at the piano whenever I sat to play. I started to look at every octave as a universe, and each key that fell within that octave was a world in its own right. Nothing was ever the same after I shifted my mind to this type of thinking. Every key has its own color and texture, which you could hear and feel. The next thing I needed to do was to understand modes, scales, and chords so I could properly explain the answer if I was asked a question.

One issue that I would come across a lot was hearing a musical phrase or a particular chord being played, and on many occasions, I would ask, "Why do you play that chord there?" or "How did you know that this particular chord would work here or is compatible here?" And the answer I would receive most times was "I felt it," "I figured it out," or "It's all God, bro." I mean, it was such an issue for me to the point where I would just record whatever it was I would hear and do my own research on it. This led me to also believe that a big difference between an untrained musician and a trained musician is that a trained musician can fully explain the reason behind their progression. They can find chords, modes, and scales, and they understand the role of whichever mode, chord, or scale that they are playing and can explain each of their functions as they relate to the song they are playing. Most untrained musicians are extremely talented and skillful, but they lack the ability to explain what it is they are doing. I think it is absolutely important that every musician takes the time not just to practice but to understand what it is he or she is playing and the roles and functions.

A lot of time, we musicians tend to take a chord progression or a phrase and apply it to another song. Sometimes it may work, and sometimes it may not. And what I have seen is some musicians cannot tell the difference because they do not understand the function of the chord or phrase played. Then they go around playing the melody or chord progression on every song they can play, and they think it is cool or applicable. And this should not be. It is very important that we understand melodies and the chord functions that go with them before interchanging them with multiple songs. I do believe the reason this happens from time to time is the lack of practice. Jam by yourself in your own time. Go through your scales and modes and understand their roles and functions. In this life, making progress does not necessarily depend on your skill level as we have seen through different life scenarios, but it's very important that the fundamentals are covered. There is no excuse for the lack of knowledge in this era.

We live in a time when we don't even need to be in a physical school to be educated. There are so many ways to learn music, it is not even funny, and therefore covering the fundamentals shouldn't be an issue. For a musician, it is of the utmost urgency that you become educated in the music you desire to pursue, especially if it is the only thing you are doing or going to do. Why do I stress this? For musicians, the job market is extremely competitive and unstable. Talent is overlooked in the blink of an eye because this world is over-populated with talented people. So even though it is important, you cannot depend on talent alone. You are going to need the education, experience, and an edge to back your talent if you should become successful in the music world. But success is measured differently through each eye that might come across it. Success could mean money, fame, connections, one-hit songs. Who knows?

Everyone has his or her version of success. I would like to ask a question. With all the one-hit wonders or the individuals who were lucky to catch a break, whether through a track or written musical work, do you still think it's essential to be trained in music? Because we know success is not tied to how educated you may be.

The next question I would like to ask is where is the line drawn in music? Is there even a line? You know, that line that lets us know whether it can logically be explained as music or not. Is it an "old school" mentality to hold on to the concepts that were once revered as the foundational principles of music? Or has it just become what it is, and we have to accept it? Things like musical lines that might have no concept are being called music, and lyrics that cannot be understood, such as "mumble rap," are being called lyrics. How do we justify or sanction their legitimacy? Is the legitimacy determined by the number of people who gravitate toward it, this new wave that is forming a face in music, or is it based on the individual's feeling of music?

Even in this facet, rivalry has shown itself between the older generation and the new generation. One side is saying that the music of today is crazy; the other side is saying the music from back then is old and outdated and does not have a place in this era. Then you have singers who cannot sing but are touring and making money versus the singers who can sing and are not touring and not making any money. You have individuals who cannot play an instrument making tracks and songs that are allowing them to be famous, go on tour, and make money versus those who have gone to school and know how to play skillfully yet are not touring or making any money. Let's not forget the Facebook, YouTube, and Instagram stars. We are now at that place where music is considered good by the number of likes, hearts, or subscriptions you receive on social media. I do know that not everyone wants to be on the road touring or desires to be in the limelight of things, but I can see how this could breathe a sense of bitterness for the way music is being perceived in today's world.

But is it because of the way music is being perceived? Or is it a lack of adaptability to move with the times? Or is it both? Because whether you agree or disagree, or you stand neutral, the fact stays that music is evolving whether we like it or not. And the way in which it will evolve is still unknown, but what I do know is if there is not a clear path as to what musical principles we will hold fast to, then who is to say what music will be in the future?

Being in music school really opened my eyes to the world

of music. Only in school do you get to really dive into cultures that you wouldn't normally associate yourself with. And most times, it's because you have to do it, knowing that your grade depends on it. Playing with individuals who are not as strong as you will definitely test your patience and show you who you are as a person. The secrets of the music world are not necessarily said or taught. It's an experience that clicks deep inside. Yes, you may learn the knowledge of what to play and why you play, but how to play and when and where you play are crucial elements that take time to master.

School shows you all of this, and it breathes life into your inner musician. Just going into a school and seeing nothing but practice rooms wherever you turn does something to your mind-set and makes you want to be more serious about your skills. It is very important that musicians go to school not just for the knowledge. Knowledge is only 25 percent of the battle. You still have 75 percent that you are responsible for, including your physical aspect, which covers dexterity and the health of your body; your personal interpretation, which covers soloing and the aesthetics of playing; and your drive and discipline, which propels you to play. But school can be an issue for some.

In this generation, you won't be able to get into a proper music school if you are not good enough. Not good enough could mean anything. The competitiveness of the music world is at an all-time high. Only the ones who stand out will be accepted. It is good, but for those who are starting late in the game, it will be a tough cookie to swallow. If you don't believe me, try getting into a good, reputable music school. The first thing you will realize is there is usually a three-stage process for the audition alone. You have to record yourself playing a swing, ballad, and one other of your choice. Then if you are accepted, you are asked to come in for a live audition to perform in front of the school music board. And last there is a written exam.

A lot of people do not understand how much pressure it is just to get into a music school. Many individuals travel across states to go through this process. Some make it through, and the rest don't and have to turn around and go home. It is really tough. But despite its difficulties, once you are in, you will quickly find out it was worth all the trouble. From the school musical staff to the students, everything breathes music, and you can't help but to fall in and be a part of it. When a part of a music school, you are constantly tested. Knowing that you are paying money to learn to hear music can be weird. Playing exactly what you are told to play can be weird seeing that it should be natural to do so. But this is not so. The discipline that comes with being in school is unlike any other, seeing that you are also graded on it. Music school is like an incubator that forces you to become mature in your skills. That's the big difference. Now I'm not knocking those who are not in school. I am trying to show how important it is to be in school.

One thing to note now is that musicians are being asked about their schooling more than ever. Like I mentioned before, it's not just about talent anymore but about the whole package. In this day and age, they want to know how long you've been playing for, whom you've worked with, and where you studied. At one point in time, if you were just good at playing, you could get a church job playing. Now, today, even the church has gone more professional in requiring musicians to be educated in what they do. Most people that I know who are extremely talented and haven't been to school are from the church. And to be honest one of the reasons why I think so many church musicians are so talented is because of the church itself. Churches have been multicultural for as long as I can remember. This is why I think church musicians are so well-versed when it comes to music. The church invites different people from all walks to be a part of their congregation, and with the people comes the culture. Musicians who attend these types of churches are forced to learn a wide variety of music, which then enhances their playing and the church services. But it doesn't always follow this particular pattern. Sometimes, church music is influenced by music outside of the church. In these cases, it could be musicians who caught a lucky break and then came back to work for the church, and their style of playing music influences it. I know a couple of individuals playing for churches who never grew up in church. But they are skilled in what they do, and they got the work done in an excellent way. But times have changed. And music jobs are becoming scarce and rare. Those who are untrained tend to be the ones who go after these kinds of jobs now, but they might lose out on these opportunities if they can't meet the requirements. It's kind of scary because the times are changing.

To teach for a school, whether public or private, the requirement is more anal. Even private tutors are being asked for degrees. It used to be if you were good, you could get a couple of kids and just teach; now, that has changed. I cannot stop to tell you how much of a negative impact this has caused on the gigs that are available. Okay, to every musician out there who is reading this right now, let me know if you can relate to this. How many times has someone called you for a gig, and the person gives the details and the requirements and then asks you how much it will cost to have you take the gig? You give the price; say, for example, you charge $400 for the gig, and the person says, "Cool. I will get back in touch with you to let you know." Now, you know you've given a fair price because you've met the requirements, you are trained, you have the skill for the gig, and it's a competitive price right across the board. You have been honest about the price.

What usually happens? Think about it. You end up getting lowballed for $150, and the gig goes to the other musician. The client calls around asking different individuals for a quote until he finds a musician who is the cheapest and will get the job done with no excellence. Sometimes the other musician who charges the $150 is not even half as skilled; he or she knows it's a fair price, but because he or she wants to get the gig, he or she will take less and will tell the client the first price is too much. I know most musicians can relate to this. For the gigs outside church, most of the time, they can't read music, are not as fluent in the style they are hired to play, have no dexterity and no longevity in soloing, and cannot close the show the way it needs to be closed. For church, the musicians can only play in one key, modulating with the transpose button. They do not know their hymns and probably won't take the time to learn them because they're old.

Now this has caused a big imbalance in the gig world, especially when it comes to the church and that is also one of the reasons why churches have musical issues because they went the cheap route. As with any business, I expect them to look around to see how they can maximize their budgets. So, I don't have a problem with that. What I have a problem with is the individuals who do not play at the level required for the gig saying that a price is too much. It causes a lot of issues when it comes to being paid as a musician because I can tell you, if any business is used to paying out a low number for a big job, then when the right musician comes around and quotes a fair price, the business is going to look at the musician like he or she is crazy. In truth, the musician is correct. But because the business is used to paying out such a low price, they won't want to move from that low budget. This is why they created the musicians' union, to help rectify these issues.

Another reason why it is important to go to music school is that it's not only the practical side of music that is being taught, but you also learn about the business side, which a lot of individuals do not know about. Learning how to monetize your music and create royalties should be the main focus of every musician. Back then, record companies would sign a lot of individuals to labels, and when it came to being paid, it was then they found out that they were screwed over by the company.

One example is the group called New Edition. They first created their five-man group in 1978 in Roxbury, Boston. Over the years, two individuals of the group left but were replaced, still keeping them as a five-man group. They later met a man named Brooke Payne who helped bring the musical talent to light by entering them in a talent show held by Maurice Starr in Boston. Though they won second place, Mr. Starr was still impressed and invited them to the studio to record. As a result, hits were created. Songs like "Is This the End?" and "Popcorn Love" did very well, and they went on tour and became a force to be reckoned with. But just as they were starting to take off, Mr. Starr's company had different plans. When they came back from tour and they were dropped off at their homes, they received a check for only $1.87, which they couldn't believe. They ended up leaving the company after suing them and were bought by MCA records. What I am really trying to say is music is not a walk in the park. It's not all fun and games. Music is a business. And we all need to understand it. Most of us barely know the business aspect of it, and we are so geared to jump in the water, but we don't know how to swim, yet school helps us in this area also.

Even in learning about the business and protecting yourself

with the tools and knowledge, you end up creating rivals. You are trying to get your share of the pie, and the record labels are trying to get their share. As the client strives to be the best, the labels strive to be in the dominant position in being the boss of all. Rivalry is all around us.

Well, it seems being trained or untrained and having rivals will never go away. The moment you decide to go after your dreams, you realize how much more preparation you need, and it shows how far behind the competition you are. Will you stop or keep moving? Will you complain about the bad hand you were dealt, or will you suck it up and make the best of it? Life has never been simple and will never be simple. One minute you are up, and the next minute you are down. It is all about how well you make decisions based on the situations you are in. Granted, there won't always be the option to pick or choose. Sometimes, you need to just jump and believe you will be okay. Some of the biggest names out there will tell you that they took a risk. We tend to shy away from jumping because we don't know what's at the bottom. But it is okay to be a little bruised at times. With that being said, wherever you are in your musical career, if you're just starting out or you feel like you're about to end, maximize your time and the possibilities to the best of your abilities. Do not stop until your goals are accomplished. And when you've reached the finish line, and you've seen how far you've come, the overwhelming joy that hits you is proof that it was worth risking everything for.

Chapter 5

The Church
versus the World

This topic has been a source of conflict since before I was even born. It is a real and very serious issue, as it pertains to the belief that, as a musician, your work and religion cannot be combined. It is frowned upon. Is this a healthy choice as a musician? What are the pros and cons in limiting yourself to one way of making music, and who ultimately benefits from the decision after it is made? Have you ever been told that music will not make you any money? Or "How dare you play music that has nothing to do with the church or that it is not 'Godly'?" On the world side, you might hear, "It sounds too churchy," "Take the seventh out of the chord," and so on. These are the types of issues that a musician might come face to face with, one way or the other. The life of the church musician can be extremely stifling to his or her growth and progress and his or her ability to be a musician. The first thing the musician is taught is the music that he or she has committed him- or herself to is sacred and holy, which is true, but what they also say is if you have committed yourself to this type of music, then you cannot play any other types of music, which is a major issue for me. Now to truly understand why music is considered "holy," we have to take a look at the "holiness movement."

The "holiness movement" is a group of beliefs and practices that stemmed from the nineteenth century, and its core doctrine is based on John Wesley's theology of a "second work of grace," which leads to Christian perfection. The second work of grace is basically a personal experience that has caused a dramatic change within the individual and removed the will to sin, which was what they believed. We know only one person is perfect, but that's another story. In addition, holy groups came together with beliefs about the moral aspects of the law of God in terms of behavioral rules—prohibiting the intake of alcohol and partaking in gambling or even something as small as going to the movie theater were frowned upon or not accepted. There were a few groups that opposed this ideology, but nevertheless, it still became a force that took over.

Now I cannot speak for anyone else, but after finding out about this particular movement, I understood where my struggle as a young musician stemmed from and where the older generation got their views from. This ideology, though it meant well, caused me to be extremely limited in my music, seeing that my early years of playing started in the church. I've been told not to use a particular sound or not to play a certain way because it sounds secular. I can remember that moment ever so vividly when I was told not to use a piano sound in church services. Only the organ was accepted or permitted because it had a sound that could be connected to reverence, or it supported the feeling that you were getting ready to enter the presence of the Lord. Yet every instrument that has been made has been used on a tour or for secular purposes. This issue has tampered with my mind for a very long time, seeing that there were no logical explanations for their request.

It's so amazing how we were created, the complexities of our unique identities, yet there is a common ground that binds all of us together. And that is our physical makeup, which makes us human. I made mention of music being pure all by itself. When listening to music, certain parts of the brain become active in order to process it. But when lyrical content is added to the music, the brain functions differently, and other parts of the brain become active, which proves that music without lyrics and music with lyrics cannot be viewed, criticized, or judged based on one's personal feelings or a one-dimensional view, which may result in an ultimatum to choose one or the other. It has to be looked at based on whether it has lyrical content or not, seeing that the brain processes the two types in different ways.

Now I would like to make a special mention of one particular lady who has influenced traditional Christian music so much, and her name is Fanny Crosby. She has been considered as the mother of gospel music with legendary hymns and poetry that we still use in our repertoire to this very day. Fanny Crosby was a blind lady who had the gift of writing music and poetry. It is said that she wrote over eight thousand hymns and songs and had over a million copies printed. "Pass Me Not, O Gentle Savior," "Blessed Assurance," and "To God Be the Glory" are just a few out of the many songs being sung in churches all over the world, even in today's generations. Though Fanny Crosby is known to be the mother of gospel music, her music did not stay only within the church.

Fanny Crosby had songs and poetry that were also popular outside of the church, which would be considered secular. Fanny Crosby cowrote secular songs with various writers and had more than five thousand recorded secular poems, which showed her versatility in the arts. Not only did she write music and poetry, but she was the one who created the first cantata by an American composer, which was also secular. It was called "The Flower Queen." The reason why I think music back then was considered holy was because they stayed within the four walls of the church. There were certain traditional styles, rhythms, and chord progressions that had to be present within the music for it to be considered holy. It was uncommon for musicians to use the secular sounds, rhythms, and tones within the church, therefore making it "unholy." Also, a common belief was anything that was used in the world was unholy for use in the church. My questions to the church are "What does it mean to be a musician through your eyes? How can you try and limit a musician to only a specific type of music?"

Now if a baby is taught the alphabet, and he or she, over a period of time, learns to develop words, will that baby only become aware of "positive" words? Or if someone who has the gift of being helpful should decide whether to help a stranger based on the stranger's beliefs, then how helpful would that individual be? I could never understand how someone can look at a musician and tell him or her, "You cannot play this type of music." Not playing his or her music would make the individual a walking contradiction to his or her talent or gifts. I found it extremely frustrating because they were literally saying the person should stop being who he or she was made to be in order to please another who, in most cases, has no clue about the world in which a musician lives.

I grew up in the era when it was looked down upon and frowned upon if you were caught playing music that wasn't gospel. I can remember clear as day the moments when it would cause an uproar to play a Kirk Franklin song in church. At that time, it was considered unholy music. I mean to the extreme level where you would be kicked out of the church for playing a song on the piano. This was around 1994 to 1999. Now, we are in the future, and I had to sit and think about how stupid those individuals must feel, now that they've lived to see how music has evolved. There's not one twenty-first-century church out there that hasn't played music in their sanctuary that has somewhat been influenced by a secular musician or secular music, whether it's a hymn or contemporary song. From Ron Kenoly to Tonex, music has gone way beyond what we could ever think.

Now I would like to take a little time at this moment to say to every single church that believes in the music and in their musicians a big thank-you. I think I can speak on behalf of every musician when I say to the churches that have pushed us to be the best we can be in our craft, we appreciate you so much. There is no way I could move forward without expressing how much you have changed our lives by investing in your musicians, whether financially or through education, and we really appreciate it. I really appreciate it. You've allowed many musicians to live out their dreams and aspirations. Some are able to start lives and have families, and we want to say thank you. I applaud your commitment to us and you not taking advantage of our gift. Not everyone wants to be on tour. Not everyone wants to travel. Some of us really want to spend the rest of our lives playing in church. But we can't do it at the sacrifice of our own lives. To be honest, most of us musicians started out just with the love for the music. It brings us joy, peace, and happiness, and all we really wanted is to be appreciated for the work that we do.

Let me just share this really quick. For some of us, if not most, we played for free for many years, and we didn't care. It wasn't about the money. It was about the place we tap into every time we touch our instrument, that place where no one exists but you and your instrument. For those who sing, it was whenever we closed our eyes and tapped into that moment. But when things started to change for me was when I started to be told how to play and what to play, and I started to be critiqued. I was just playing because I loved it. But for those churches who stand by their musicians, I thank you from the bottom of my heart. The church means well at times, but their views on their musicians are somewhat screwed. Currently, it has greatly improved with the times that we live in. But there is still a sense that musicians should play for the church and play for free. Some have even gone on to say that if your skills are considered to be in the beginner level, then your playing should be free. If you're playing on a consistent level for the church, you should be compensated, whether you're a professional or a beginner. How much? That should be determined over a conversation, but if you're playing every week, something should be done financially. If the church doesn't think you are worthy or at the level to be considered for payment, then you should simply not play. This is what I believe. I say get as much training as you can, and practice your heart out. When you reach a level where you can be recognized and paid, then you can go back to the playing field. This does not appy to babies in the field. So many times, musicians are told they need to practice more, or "You need to become more professional. You need to have your degree before you can be paid by the church, but yet the church would still use the same musicians to play for services, banquets, and various event while telling them to get their skills up to be paid. So, in other words, they are good enough to play for free but not good enough to be paid. Yikes ... not cool.

One of the most demanding jobs in a church that is dangerously underestimated is the job of a musician. Whether you work with the choir or the instruments, it tends to be one of the most underestimated by the church, yet it is extremely demanding. Another big issue that the church musician struggles with is the fact the church tends to forget that music has a direct correlation with muscle memory, rhythmic patterns, and the physical and mental ability to sing or play, and yet they expect you to make the impossible possible by putting individuals in choirs who do not possess the talent and placing musicians who cannot play in these crucial positions.

Now I do understand the choir is also a ministry. It gives a sense of hope, and it makes people feel like they belong to a family that is forged over a period of time. But the fundamental goal of the choir is for singing, not so that people can feel a sense of security. Then, if the musician should give his or her professional opinion on removing the individuals who can't sing or play, in most cases, the musician is reprimanded because of political ties the individual might have in the church or because of the influence he or she might poses in the church. If the person who does not know how to play or sing is a family member of the pastor, he or she may be given special privileges.

I personally was reprimanded for not allowing a person to join the choir. She was a newcomer, and she expressed how she had always sung from the time she was a young girl and now she wanted to have the opportunity to sing at our church because where she was coming from she was singing on the choir. I said, "Great! Let's set up a day for an audition, and we will take it from there."

I had my choir leader in place for the audition, and we began. At first, we were a little taken aback by what we heard because she told us she was a singer, and she had been sing-ing for years. But what I and the choir leader heard did not support her assertion of having sung for years. We gave her as much time as we could, and she was given the liberty to choose her best song to sing, but what we heard was not good. After she was finished, I sat with her asked why she wanted to be on the choir. She said she'd always wanted to be on the choir, and everyone told her how great of a singer she was, but she didn't pursue it, so she decided to try at this point in her life. I respectfully said, "Though your attempt is honest and pure, and I know you really want to sing with your whole heart, I think in my professional opinion you should get some help to improve on your fundamental elements of singing. At this time, we cannot take you on. But we are willing to help with training or we can direct you in the right direction."

She did not take it lightly and took an offense to us letting her know our decision. And she went away and did not attend the church after.

Now the reason why I mention this example was because these issues happen quite often, maybe not this particular issue, but similar ones happen more than you will ever know. First thing is, she was an older lady in the church who had just lost her husband after many years with him, so she was a widow. During her counseling session with one of our pastors, she was asked what it was that brought her happiness, and she said singing. And just like that, she was instructed to join the choir. Without any thought of whether or not she could sing on a choir, it was okay for her to join the choir. When I took the time to evaluate the situation, it showed me the lack of respect we have toward the choir. I sometimes think that the purpose of the choir is solely to show the number of members on the choir and not for the purpose of singing. I mean, why is it okay for just anyone to join? Am I the only one who sees this as an issue? The second thing was no one took the time to evaluate the emotional state of the lady to see if this was the best move for her.

Third, no one spoke to the musician (me) to let me know the full details of the reason why she was instructed to join the choir. I would have suggested working with her on a one-on-one basis to properly evaluate the situation.

Fourth, my main concern, she was not asked to join the choir based on her ability to sing or her ability to function in a musical setting but for emotional stability as part of the grieving process.

There have been many occasions where the church has used the ministry as a therapy session. I am all for helping people who may need a little help using music, but I am against just throwing them into the main heartbeat of the church, seeing that it has a direct impact on the flow of service. Hurt people only bring more hurt unless they take the time to deal with the issues that are causing the hurt.

Another major problem that I've come across on multiple occasions in working with churches is that the pastor's family is often heavily involved in the music ministry. I cannot begin to tell you how crazy this can be. From singers to pianists to drummers to bass players, to ministers, sound engineers, and so on, you name it. This is a major problem.

People being given a responsibility solely on the basis that they are the son or daughter of someone, and their not being capable to fulfill the basic necessary duties that are required seriously puts the ministry at a disadvantage for growth.

For example, I have had to work with individuals who do not have any interest in drums. They do not practice. They do not invest in their craft to elevate their skills. They do not even own a drum, which would be the first thing any drummer who is serious would desire, yet based solely on the premises of the relationship to the head, they are at their free will to do as they like, or better yet, play as they like without any re-percussions. I have worked with individuals who cannot sing to save their life. Even worse, the individuals are praised by their pastors about how great of a job they are doing, which solidifies their resolve.

Sometimes I wonder if I'm in the same world as the pastors who are giving the praise, because I'm like, *No way, there's no way what I'm hearing and what you the pastor are hearing is the same thing.* I had to accept the hard reality that we live in a world where anything can be considered great just because its in the church. Let's forget about the spiritual part for a moment. I have yet to meet a pastor who asked, "What steps are you taking for your skills to reach the next level? What are you doing? Are you practicing? Are you taking classes that affect your growth in playing, dancing, and singing?" Yet they praise these individuals and critique their talents without knowing if the musicians, dancers, and singers are failing and if the ministry is dying. They give these individuals seats at the top in roles that determine the growth and the health of the music ministry based on relationship and not on their ability to do the job or even their ability to sing, dance, or even play. It's extremely hilarious when you hear the reasoning behind which roles were given to the individuals. Some said it "keeps them out of trouble," it "keeps them in church," or they might lack the ability to sing or play, but their life is "holy." And the best one of all, they might not play or sing or dance well, but they are anointed. I mean it's so preposterous the response you might get, yet the church is "loyal to their demise," and I cannot shake the hypocrisy in the whole scheme of things because the church has always been the first one to point fingers when their musicians leave to play on tour and start to make a little money. Out of nowhere, the individuals are playing for the devil. I mean no one sees the devil in the chaotic structure within the ministry, within their four walls. The devil is right in front of your nose, and you still can't see it. But yet we are the ones who are unholy if we play for a big artist who is secular. And if playing with individuals who take their craft seriously is considered unholy, then put me down as unholy also. I will always choose to play with people who are serious about the craft and can execute the job that needs to be done. I will always choose to do my job the right way even from a structural point of view. It is imperative. The structure is what will determine the growth of anything.

As a matter of fact, I personally would chose to work outside rather than inside the church because the structure makes more sense outside the church. Yes, you might say that's because of financial backing, and spiritual protocal, though that might be a point, it still comes down to the structure. You cannot choose a triangle expecting it to fill a slot that has four sides. Wouldn't you need a square for that? Then how can we place people in these positions knowing that they do not have the skill needed to fit them. *It is simple.* A drummer needs to play drums, a singer needs to sing, a pianist needs to play piano, and a bass player needs to play bass. And when I say "needs to play," I mean they must possess at least the fundamental requirements of the three respective instruments to be proficient. There are no ways around it.

How can a musician make music under these conditions? A musician cannot make music under these conditions, and if he or she can't make music, then it affects him or her in ways you will never understand. It is extremely unfair. As a musician, if you are not careful, you will be fired for the very thing you got hired to do! Do you know how hard it is in the twenty-first century for a church to survive without music? I would even dare to go as far as stating that within any twenty-first-century megachurch, you will find the music ministry is at the heart of that church. Thank God that these churches understand the importance of a strong music ministry, which includes getting strong musicians. But the sad reality is, not every church has this progressive mind-set. Some churches are stuck in their ways and do not want to shift their mind-sets to the next level, which is getting professionals to do the job with excellency—a whole other issue on its own.

There was a friend of mine who got into some trouble with his church because he was asked to play at a secular gig. It was an awesome opportunity he had, and he had so much fun he ended up singing, which is funny because he cannot sing. But word got back to his pastor about him being out and performing with his friends, and apparently the pastor was not necessarily elated by the news. The pastor called a meeting with the musician, wanting to figure out what made him decide to play out at a secular gig. The musician stated that his friends had asked him to play for them, which he didn't see a problem with. *No biggie*, he thought. He also stated that he wanted to do it because it was fun. The pastor told the musician that the double-standard life he was living was a serious concern for him and the church. He said to the musician that he could only play for the "Lord" or the "church," and to play for any other reason was a sinful act. The pastor's reasoning was as follows: if you as a musician go out and play for a person who sings or plays music that makes people dance and sing and think in a perverted way, then you are aiding or you are also responsible for the outcome. The pastor didn't want the musician to be associated with the world. I laughed so hard because that is just impossible.

I asked my musician friend, "How did you end up playing for this type of pastor?"

He stated that he was at a wedding gig playing, and the pastor approached him afterward. I asked, "Was the wedding at a church?" He said no. I asked, "Were you playing any gospel or church song at the time of the wedding?" He said no. I turned to him and shook my head because here you have a pastor who left the church to go and search for a musician outside the church. Not only did he find a musician playing secular music at the time of his search, but he went up to him, acknowledged his skills, and then offered him a job.

Now the same pastor is trying to take a stand with the musician about how important it is to the church that he not play secular music? What did he think would happen? That he would only play church music? What do you think happens when a musician goes to music school and studies? Does the church even know the history of music? Does the church even know how many hours we spend in a class sitting down, constantly listening to libraries of secular music, transcribing music, and breaking music apart to understand its foundation? How can you try to undo what is bred in us, what we were born to do? How do you think we would perceive your talk about only playing for church when we study for years in a classroom, with teachers shouting and screaming at us, drilling us over and over about time signatures, finger positioning, vocal exercise, dance flexibilities and routines, the history of jazz and classical music, and the individuals who change the way we even see and play music to this day? How can you try to limit us with lack of knowledge and segregated beliefs? Do you know what it means to play until your fingers hurt or even bleed? Do you know what it means for a dancer to ache in pain trying to perfect a piece, yet you disregard and minimize the sacrifice of the art? Yet you need us. This is wrong and extremely offensive.

Now if we were to cut the cake right down the middle and be completely open and honest, then everyone should be held responsible. If the church is going to judge and point fingers about the type of music musicians play on their own time, then you have to judge everyone who works or does something for a living. So many people work for companies in America that do not support their belief system; yet they do it for the money, and they are not criticized about their job. What would you say to an actor who might have a kissing scene in a show? What would you say to a person who works in law enforcement and has to lock people up based on a quota and not based on a law that was broken? Is the policeman not a Christian because he is a police officer? Is the actor not a Christian because she is an actor? So, why is it that we are so heavily criticized for doing the very thing we were born to do? A musician's job is to make and play music, not just one type of music but music on the whole.

I honestly think the church needs to reevaluate their hiring process. What I have seen in my time as a musician is that the church is the first to talk about being holy and righteous about playing, but they accept anyone at the cheapest rate inside of the ministry.

After you go the cheap route, then you mandate the musician pay tithes into the church. Can I say something? The moment it becomes a mandate, it's no longer effective. It becomes taxing, because tithing is predicated on how you give. It's based on your heart. So, for those churches that automatically take tithes out of a musician's check, be warned that it will not be helpful to you. Most times, musicians are not properly evaluated on their history. In fact, most times, in the hiring process, the church has no clue whom they are in the midst of. It could be a killer, a rapist, someone with multiple families or babies all over the place, or someone with a different belief system that is totally contrary to their teaching. They could be hiring an atheist all because they are so eager to get a musician. It's kind of crazy because it wasn't the norm to have background checks being done on the musicians coming in. And I'm sure you all can testify that not everyone who has claimed the Lord as his or her savior is really saved. Not only that, but the times are changing. People are coming into the church and killing people off in the church, literally.

This in itself is a problem. Not only do you expose the church to an attack on the name of the organization, but you also expose your members to physical, spiritual, emotional, and mental attack if the wrong individual comes in as a musician. Even the way you terminate the musicians is crazy. Okay, you know you're having issues with the musician, and you wait until after the fourth service or after the busiest time or season on the church calendar to tell him or her not to come back. So, you use the musician to your advantage and kick him or her to the curb. It's crazy how we treat each other.

When we first came in for an interview, we went through the process and closed with a prayer. When you're about to fire us, you do it through a text. We are lucky if we get a phone call, but one thing is for sure, you do not send us out with prayer or kind words. Most definitely, this way of functioning cannot be healthy. If you're going to teach, preach, and create change, then it has to start with you. Because it's not how we start with the prayer that counts but how you end with the prayer.

For us as musicians, we need to get a lot more serious about what we do. We take these church gigs, and we make a mess of the job we sign a contract to do. We show up late, and we are unprofessional with the way we walk or talk. We give our words to show up for a gig, and because another gig pops up paying more money, we go back on our word and leave the church high and dry after we've made the commitment. We have lost our honor and integrity while failing to uphold our end of the bargain. We go around sleeping with all the women as men, and the female musicians go around sleeping with all these men, and we destroy the relationship between the church and the music. Some of us don't know how to read music, how to teach parts, how to construct a simple three- or four-part harmony or to put people in their correct sections in the choir, how to keep a steady time in our element, or how to play pocket or straight. Some of us do not know our keys, chord progression, or theory. Some of us do not know how to sing a dissonance or sing without doing a riff, or we have no repertoire of vocal style or even exercises, and yet we think it's right to charge these ridiculous prices coming onto a gig. We as musicians are crazy. How can we really think our actions are justified? Most of us come in with a lot of baggage and expect the church to pay the bill on that baggage, and if they don't, we want to act up and raise our voice, but we have yet to show any sense of loyalty. We haven't shown that the job is more than a check, and we come with an expectation that the church owes us something. We as musicians need to stop. It is only going to make things worse.

We need to find a healthy way to sit as musicians with the church to talk and mend the broken areas between us. There needs to be an open and neutral ground to hit every important point that affects both sides, so we rectify the issues at hand.

I have personally taken church gigs in which I met with their choirs and singers, we would rehearse two times a week for three weeks in advance before the show or event, and at the end of the show, they would give the musicians $100 each with a "God bless you." Yet they would get a big-time preacher and pay him or her a lot of money (depending on the name) for a thirty- to forty-minute word. Now in my experience, most guest preachers miss the praise and worship segment. They come in time for the offering and preaching, yet the musicians play right through the service. The musicians play for the praise and worship, play through the prayer and the welcome, and play for the selections, the offertory, and the altar call and in the preaching segment. Just to go a step further, some preachers do not preach without music. Yet we are one of the most abused, underrated, and underestimated ministries in the church. So why should a church musician stay under these conditions? Isn't it ironic that most of the musicians out there who have played with the big names came from the church or had affiliations with the church? We tend to wonder why a church musician would cross over. Can I also go as far as to say that the musician who grew up in the church and has crossed over tends not to cross back over to the church after he or she leaves? Why is that? Based on my experience, I would say the number one reason for church musicians to leave is because the church does not put a high value on their musicians. The world, in contrast, understands the value and the importance of a musician, and they treat musicians better than most churches will ever do.

Everything in entertainment has music as a foundational pillar built in its structure. Even corporate America has adopted music in its structure by adding music to elevators and to the phone line so you can listen to music as you wait. So why is it that the church mistreats and misuses musicians? It's a sad reality that the church will lose a part of their foundational pillar not because of lack of knowledge but because of traditional beliefs that are not even biblical. There is nothing more gratifying, nothing more addicting, nothing more fulfilling than knowing that you are working with like-minded musicians who are just as skillful and serious about the very music they are working on. Most churches will not have the level of music they require because they are really not serious about the music or they do not fully understand its significance. The church has dropped the ball when it comes to the growth of the musician by allowing personal issues and political ties to get involved with the music.

I have turned down gigs paying $4,500 a month being a church pianist knowing the headache that will come with working there as their musician. Sometimes it's not about the money but the music. I do believe because of the outside requirements where music is concerned, a lot of musicians will leave at the first opportunity they get. Not only do they get the opportunity, but the outside pays on top of it. Do I agree that a musician should leave the church and go secular? Hmm. Not necessarily. Being a musician is about maturing in your skills. Different experiences are also essential to shape one's playing styles.

One of the biggest struggles I had in honing my craft was I tried to play everything I knew in one song. Whether it called for it or not, I wanted to show or prove that I knew things and I could keep up. I wanted to show I had style, and I could do "licks" or phrases. And sometimes it gets the best of us as musicians. I do not know one musician who hasn't gone through this. I am a firm believer in practicing your craft. Make time to study and practice your instrument. It will only help your future. This is why musicians shed so much. It's like a big musical think tank where we come together and just play our ideas out. Whether they execute it correctly or not, it's almost like a safe zone to a certain degree.

Back in the nineties, I would sit and listen to a tape deck or CD player, and if I missed a chord or phrase, I would have to rewind over and over until I got it. It was a long and tedious process, but it was worth it. Now we have YouTube with free tutorials to teach us so much within a short time. We don't have to sit and rewind as much because we can look online and find the answers. There is no excuse for lack of knowledge in this era. Hope is nothing until you start to work toward the thing you are hoping for. There are certain skills you must learn and the church might not possess the resources to support you. I can say that a few churches still try to hold on to the negative type of thinking, that you should play as a service unto the Lord. But most churches have come a long way. More churches have started to take care of their musicians not only in supplying financial support but by training them to be the best they can be. We are so grateful for them, like I said. And it's churches like these that make us want to stay in church not because we get paid, but because we need to know we are appreciated and not taken for granted.

Pastors, when was the last time you stopped and just prayed for the band and the singers? Did it ever occur to you that the service was directly linked to the responsibilities of the musicians? Okay, here's is another question. When was the last time you had a service in which you prayed for everyone in the church, and the musicians were included, or when you've invited the church up to the altar, the musicians were also included? So many times, I've sat and watched everyone go up and get prayed for while we played and played. Pastors would come down into the audience and touch and pray for everyone while the musicians are playing and working. But I always wondered why we were left out. It's almost like we were robots during that part of the service. Can you think for a second just how you would feel if the musician should mess up in the highest spiritual part of the service? Man. The looks, the verbal comments, and the person with the mic might even stress the frustration verbally, causing an embarrassing moment. Everyone expects us to function, to know the mind of the speaker/pastor/prophet/apostle, and to just "flow" in the spirit. We are expected to know the right song at the right time to sing it. It's almost robotic the way in which we are expected to function, yet after all the shouting and screaming is done, no one remembers the musicians. They want to talk about our dressing and want to express to us how important it is to be more involved, yet they wonder why it is we won't let them in our world.

References

Ament, Aharona. "Beyond Vibrations: The Deaf Experience in Music." *Gapersblock*, July 22, 2010, http://gapersblock. com/transmission/2010/07/22/beyond_vibrations_the_ deaf_musical_experience/.

Kimble, Drew. "Five Fears that Can Destroy an Artist." Skinny Artist, https://skinnyartist.com/5-fears-that-can-destroy-an-artist/.

"The Three Biggest Fears Musicians Struggle With." That Sweet Roar. http://www.inspiredtosing.com/blog/the-3-biggest-fears-musicians-face.

WISE Channel. "Feel the Music: Deaf Children Sense Sounds in Switzerland (Learning World: S5E20, 3/3)." YouTube

video, 3:56. February 26, 2015, https://www.youtube.
com/watch?v=CDpE1ajC4mo.

http://drugaware.com.au/getting-the-facts/
faqs-ask-a-question/what-are-drugs/#what-is-a-drug